**Introd**

E                                                                    e

Raintree

Raintree is an imprint of Capstone Global Library Limited, a company incorporated in England and Wales having its registered office at 7 Pilgrim Street, London, EC4V 6LB – Registered company number: 6695582

www.raintreepublishers.co.uk
myorders@raintreepublishers.co.uk

Text © Capstone Global Library Limited 2014
First published in hardback in 2014
Paperback edition first published in 2015
The moral rights of the proprietor have been asserted.

Edited by Dan Nunn, Rebecca Rissman, Sian Smith, and Helen Cox Cannons
Designed by Philippa Jenkins
Original illustrations © Capstone Global Library Ltd 2014
Picture research by Liz Alexander and Tristan Leverett
Production by Vicki Fitzgerald
Originated by Capstone Global Library Ltd
Printed and bound in China by Leo Paper Products Ltd

ISBN 978 1 406 26297 1 (hardback)
17 16 15 14 13
10 9 8 7 6 5 4 3 2 1

ISBN 978 1 406 26306 0 (paperback)
18 17 16 15 14
10 9 8 7 6 5 4 3 2 1

British Library Cataloguing in Publication Data
Oxlade, Chris
Introducing Europe. – (Introducing continents)
A full catalogue record for this book is available from the British Library.

## Acknowledgements

The author and publisher are grateful to the following for permission to reproduce copyright material: Alamy p. 19 (© Eye Ubiquitous); Getty Images pp. 16 (Flickr/ Rob Kints), 18 (John Howard/Riser), 26 (Mark A Leman/Stone); naturepl.com p. 14 (© Tom Mangelsen); Shutterstock pp. 6 (© Maugli), 7 (© Bill Poon), 8 (© Prometheus72), 9 (© Johann Helgason), 11 (© Vladimir Mucibabic), 12 (© Wild Arctic Pictures), 13 (© tovovan), 15 (© FotoVeto), 17 (© Foodpictures), 20 (© chantal de bruijne), 21 (© Sergey Petrov), 23 (© AND Inc.), 24 (© Anastasios71), 25 (© Kletr), 27 (© Natalia Mikhaylova); SuperStock p. 10 (Axiom Photographic Limited).

Cover photographs of a beautiful lake in the Danube Delta, Romania and a shaded relief map of Europe reproduced with permission of Shutterstock (© Porojnicu Stelian, © Vitoriano Jr.); image of a cafe at the market square of Greifswald, Germany reproduced with permission of SuperStock (© F1 ONLINE).

Every effort has been made to contact copyright holders of material reproduced in this book. Any omissions will be rectified in subsequent printings if notice is given to the publisher.

## Disclaimer

All the internet addresses (URLs) given in this book were valid at the time of going to press. However, due to the dynamic nature of the internet, some addresses may have changed, or sites may have changed or ceased to exist since publication. While the author and publisher regret any inconvenience this may cause readers, no responsibility for any such changes can be accepted by either the author or the publisher.

# Contents

Some words are shown in bold, **like this**. You can find out what they mean by looking in the glossary.

# About Europe

Europe is one of the world's seven **continents**. A continent is a huge area of land. Europe is the second smallest of the continents. The eastern side of Europe is connected to Asia, the largest continent.

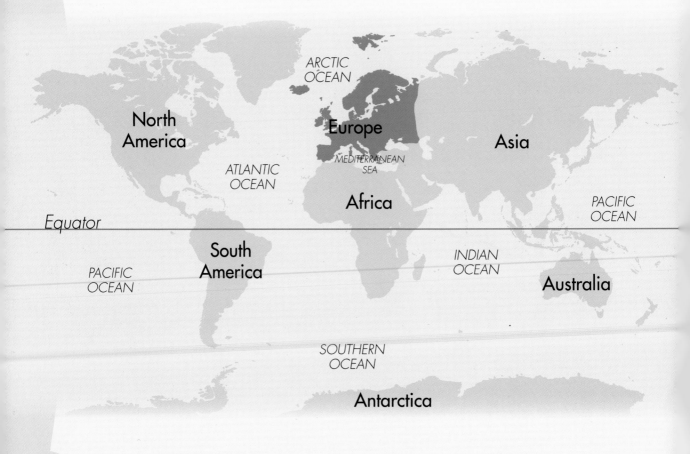

North America

ARCTIC OCEAN

Europe

Asia

ATLANTIC OCEAN

MEDITERRANEAN SEA

Africa

PACIFIC OCEAN

Equator

South America

PACIFIC OCEAN

INDIAN OCEAN

Australia

SOUTHERN OCEAN

Antarctica

The Atlantic Ocean lies to the west of Europe. The Mediterranean Sea lies to the south. To the north is the Arctic Ocean. There are many islands in these oceans that are part of Europe.

| Europe fact file | |
| --- | --- |
| Area | 9,938,000 square kilometres (3,837,081 square miles) |
| Population | 740 million |
| Number of countries | 49 |
| Highest mountain | Mount Elbrus at 5,642 metres (18,510 feet) |
| Longest river | River Volga at 3,700 kilometres (2,229 miles) |

# Famous places

There are many famous places in Europe. The Colosseum in Rome, Italy, is a huge **arena** that was built almost 2,000 years ago. Romans went to the Colosseum to see gladiators fight each other.

The Colosseum is one of the most popular places to visit in Europe.

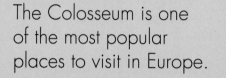

The Eiffel Tower is 324 metres (1,063 feet) tall.

The Eiffel Tower is the most famous building in Paris, France. Millions of people go to the top every year. Buckingham Palace in London and Red Square in Moscow, Russia are other famous places to visit.

# Geography

There are many **mountain ranges** in Europe.
The Alps are more than 1,126 kilometres (700 miles)
long. They stretch from France to Austria. Europe's
highest mountain is Mount Elbrus in the
Caucasus Mountains.

Mont Blanc is the highest mountain in the Alps.

This photograph shows one of Iceland's volcanoes erupting.

There are some **active volcanoes** in Europe. Mount Etna is on the island of Sicily, in Italy. It erupts every few years. There are more than 30 active volcanoes in Iceland. There are also hot springs and **geysers**.

The Volga is the longest river in Europe. The Rhine and the Danube flow through the middle of Europe. Ships carry **cargo** between cities on these rivers. The Danube flows through nine different countries.

The River Danube flows through Budapest in Hungary.

Lake Onega
Lake Ladoga
Lake Peipus
Lake Vänern
Lake Vättern
Lake Geneva
Lake Lucerne
Lake Balaton

0 250 miles
0 400 km

Chillon castle stands on the shores of Lake Geneva in Switzerland.

Europe has many large lakes. Lake Ladoga in Russia is the largest lake. It is 219 kilometres (136 miles) across. There are beautiful lakes in the mountains of Switzerland and Italy. Finland has thousands of lakes.

# Weather

Europe has many different types of weather. In the far north, it is always cold and icy. It is so cold that the sea is frozen solid. Even in the middle of summer the temperature is only just above freezing.

Snow and ice cover the far north of Europe.

Around the Mediterranean Sea in the south of Europe, the weather is hot and sunny in summer. In most of Europe, summer is warm and winter is cool. It can be rainy at any time of year.

# Animals

Polar bears, seals, and reindeer live in the cold **Arctic** parts of Europe. Wolves, bears, deer, and foxes are some of the animals that live in the huge forests in the north of Europe.

Arctic foxes grow a thick white coat in winter.

The great spotted woodpecker lives in Europe's woodlands.

Golden eagles fly in Europe's hills and mountains. Beautiful flamingos, pelicans, and many other sorts of birds live in the **delta** of the River Danube. Otters live in rivers, lakes, and along the coast.

# Plants and other living things

In the far north of Europe, mosses and **lichens** grow on the frozen **tundra**. There are also forests of conifer trees, such as pine trees and fir trees. Further south are forests of **deciduous** trees, such as oaks and beeches.

These snow-covered forests are in the far north of Europe.

These olive trees are growing on a farm in Turkey.

Different sorts of plants grow in the far south, where the weather is warmer and drier. There are olive trees, lemon trees, and orange trees. There are also vineyards full of grape vines.

# People

About 738 million people live in Europe. There are many different groups of people, such as Russians, Turks, and Finns. Millions of people from the world's other **continents** live in Europe, too.

People from different parts of the world mix together in European cities.

BAYONNE - BAIONA

i P CENTRE VILLE
HIRI BARNEA
Hôtel de Ville - Herriko Etxea
Police - Polizategia

Chapelle Impériale

PLAGES - HONDARTZAK

In the southwest of France, the road signs are in French and a language called Basque.

Most countries in Europe have their own language. In some countries, different groups of people speak different languages. People in Switzerland speak German, French, or Italian.

# Culture

Football is the most popular sport in Europe. Millions of people play it themselves or watch teams such as Manchester City, AC Milan, or Real Madrid. Cycling, rugby, and handball are also very popular.

The Tour de France is the world's most famous cycle race.

These ballet dancers are on stage at the famous Bolshoi Theatre in Moscow.

There are many famous art galleries in Europe, including the Louvre in Paris, France, and the Uffizi Gallery in Florence, Italy. Visitors can see beautiful paintings and sculptures. There are also many famous theatres and opera houses.

# Countries

Altogether there are 49 countries in Europe. Russia is easily the largest country, even though only part of Russia is in Europe. The rest is in Asia. The Vatican City in Rome is the smallest country. It is also the smallest country in the world.

This map shows the countries of Europe.

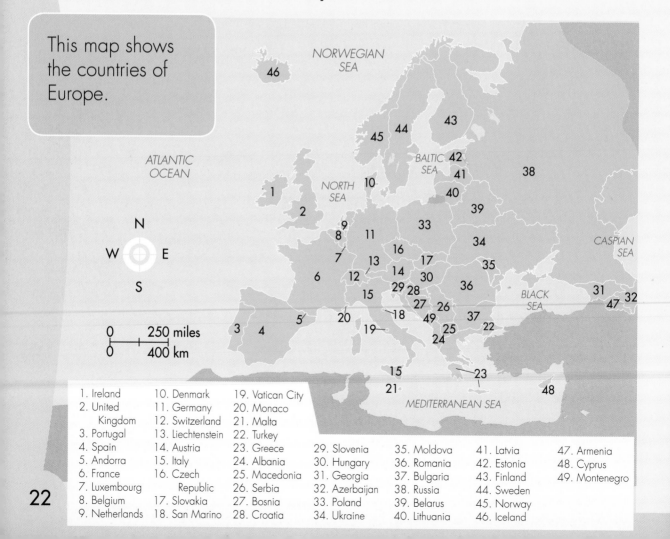

1. Ireland
2. United Kingdom
3. Portugal
4. Spain
5. Andorra
6. France
7. Luxembourg
8. Belgium
9. Netherlands
10. Denmark
11. Germany
12. Switzerland
13. Liechtenstein
14. Austria
15. Italy
16. Czech Republic
17. Slovakia
18. San Marino
19. Vatican City
20. Monaco
21. Malta
22. Turkey
23. Greece
24. Albania
25. Macedonia
26. Serbia
27. Bosnia
28. Croatia
29. Slovenia
30. Hungary
31. Georgia
32. Azerbaijan
33. Poland
34. Ukraine
35. Moldova
36. Romania
37. Bulgaria
38. Russia
39. Belarus
40. Lithuania
41. Latvia
42. Estonia
43. Finland
44. Sweden
45. Norway
46. Iceland
47. Armenia
48. Cyprus
49. Montenegro

The European Parliament building is in the city of Strasbourg, France.

Twenty-seven countries in Europe are members of a group called the European Union (EU). The countries work together to help each other. The European Union makes laws that must be followed in the different countries.

# Cities and countryside

There are many big cities in Europe. London, Moscow, and Paris are three of the biggest. They are the capital cities of the United Kingdom, Russia, and France. Only one half of the city of Istanbul, in Turkey, is in Europe. The other half is in Asia.

There are ancient buildings in Athens, the capital city of Greece.

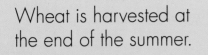
Wheat is harvested at the end of the summer.

In the countryside, farmers grow crops and raise animals such as cattle, sheep, and pigs. Wheat is the most common crop. It is used to make bread and pasta. In the far north of Europe, it is too cold to grow crops.

# Natural resources and products

Europe has many **natural resources**. Wood is harvested from the forests of northern Europe. New trees are planted to replace the ones that are cut down. Coal is an important fuel. It is dug from the ground in Russia, Germany, and Poland.

This oil rig in the North Sea pumps oil from under the seabed.

There are many car-making factories in Europe. Famous makes of car made here are Volkswagen, BMW, and Citroën. There is also a big fashion industry. Fashion shows take place in Paris, Milan, and London.

# Fun facts

- The Caspian Sea is the world's biggest lake, but it is called a sea because it is full of saltwater.

- The coast of Norway has many deep valleys filled by seawater that reach far inland. They are called fjords (say "fee-yords").

- Venice is a city in Italy that is built on islands. There are canals instead of streets, and people travel around by boat.

- In some parts of the Netherlands, the land is below the level of the sea. The sea is held back by giant banks and dams.

# Quiz

1. Which is the longest river in Russia?

2. Which two countries are half in Europe and half in Asia?

3. What is Etna? And where is it?

4. What is the most popular sport in Europe?

4. Football

3. It's a volcano, on the island of Sicily in Italy

2. Russia and Turkey

1. The Volga

# Glossary

**active volcano** mountain with a hole in the top which ash or hot melted rock comes out of

**Arctic** area of Earth around the North Pole, where it is always cold

**arena** a building where sports events and other events are held

**cargo** anything carried by a ship, lorry, or plane, such as coal, oil, stone, or goods such as cars, fridges, or computers

**continent** one of seven huge areas of land on Earth

**deciduous** tree that loses its leaves in winter

**delta** area shaped like a triangle where a river splits and flows into the sea

**geyser** natural fountain of hot water and steam, made by hot rocks under the ground

**lichen** simple plants that grow on the bark of trees, on rock, and on walls

**mountain range** large group of mountains

**natural resources** natural materials that we use, such as wood, coal, oil, and rock

**tundra** large area of flat land with no trees near the Arctic

# Find out more

## Books

*Europe* (Exploring Continents), Jane Bingham (Heinemann Library, 2008)

*Horrible Geography of the World*, Anita Ganeri (Scholastic, 2010)

*Oxford First Atlas* (OUP, 2010)

## Websites to visit

**kids.discovery.com/tell-me/people-and-places/our-7-continents**
Games, puzzles, and activities about the seven continents can be found on this website.

**kids.nationalgeographic.com/kids/games/geographygames/copycat**
This fun game helps you to find the continents on a map of the world.

**www.worldatlas.com**
This site has lots of maps, facts, and figures about continents.

# Index